by Wendell "Hurricane" Fite
with Wiley "Shark" Griffin and Jean Givan

This Book is Dedicated to the Memory of:
Jason "Jam Master Jay" Mizell and
Adam "MCA" Yauch

The information contained in this book is for informational purposes only.

I give my opinion based on my own personal experience. If you need professional advice, seek that advice.

No part of this book shall be produced, transmitted or sold in whole or in part in any form, without prior written consent of the authors.

Readers of this book are advised to do their own due diligence when it comes to making business and life decisions. All information should be independently verified by your own qualified professionals. By reading this book, you agree that Wendell "Hurricane" Fite, Wiley "Shark" Griffin and Jean Givan are not responsible for the success or failure of your life and/or business related to any information provided in this book.

Contents

INTRODUCTION

The Right Place at the Right Time

Being born in the middle of the 1960's when the Vietnam War was in full effect, turbulence and civil unrest gripped many segments of society protesting the war, injustice, police brutality, poverty and racism, all while the Civil Rights Movement was heating up, sprinkled in between the assassinations of President John F. Kennedy; his brother, the Attorney General, Robert F. Kennedy; famed Civil Rights Leader, Dr. Martin Luther King, Jr. and Black Muslim Militant, Malcolm X, did not seem like the best time to not only manage to have dreams but to somehow find a way to make those dreams come true.

I was originally born in Dallas, Texas, and 3 years old when my mom left my dad. She had packed all her kids (my 2 sisters and 3 brothers), and drove to New York and we wound up living on 110th Avenue and 205th Street in Hollis, Queens – New York.

Hollis Hot

I grew up in Hollis – in the midst (and in the shadows) of the ground-breaking hip hop kings,RunDMC (with my childhood and lifelong buddy, their DJ, Jam Master Jay – may he RIP), the most widely known hip hop advocate and spokesman, Russell Simmons, and at an early age, I had constant exposure to hip hop legends.

RunDMC gave Hollis, Queens legitimacy in the then up and coming hip hop culture which was first started in the Bronx. But there were others in Hollis who have done major things in hip hop. Kurtis Blow's DJ (Davy D) and I formulated a group known as Solo Sounds; Ed Lover had his own crew, Master Sounds.

LL Cool J is from St. Albans which is right next to Hollis. Some other Queens notables who made their mark in hip hop are: Salt 'N Pepa (originally known as Super Nature, and their DJ, Spindarella), Nas, Roxanne Shante, Kid 'N Play, a Tribe Called Quest and the Lost Boys, to name a few. Years later, 50 Cents and JaRule emerged from Queens' hip hop elite, as well as Irv Gotti, another Queens native who became a legend in the world of hip hop.

In my young Hollis days, I met a guy named Mark, who lived on 212th Street and Hollis Avenue.He left an impression on me when I went to his house and saw himbackspinning 45's (the small records), real fast. I had never seen that before. Mark would later become known as "the 45 King" and hook up with Queen Latifah and the Flavor Unit.

Good Lookin' Out, Sis

There were lots of crews popping up as the hip hop culture emerged. I was in it for the fun. It was challenging and very exciting. While people were playing Pac Man, Centipede, Space Invaders and trying to master the Rubik's Cube, I was making cassette tapes on boom boxes and hitting the turntables. My sister (who could DJ very well) had DJ equipment that I practiced on, and I honed my skills.

My sister had an outdoor birthday party that got rained-out. So they moved all the DJ equipment to the garage. Days later, I returned to my big sister's garage and practiced on the turntables, fostering my skills that I still use today.

From Hot to Shot

I'd be misleading you bigtime if I said I had a dream and poof, I accomplished it. No, there was struggle. And sometimes I made decisions which could have easily cost me my life, or derailed me. For example, when I got older, I was part of a group of guys from my neighborhood known as the Hollis Crew who had gone up to Andrew Jackson High School to help my childhood buddy Jam Master Jay after he an altercation with a Five Percenter (a member of a group who believe that the original black man is God and consider themselves to be a nation of Gods and Earths).

Quite a few of us from Hollis had been ejected from our local public high school, Andrew Jackson, because of our bad behavior back then. But Jay was a good guy and he was still going to Jackson, and he and was outnumbered by a bunch of Five Percenters.

About 50 of us from the Hollis Crew walked into Andrew Jackson High School, coming from all different directions. A guy I didn't know very well named Ronnie Mack who I had somehow attached himself to the crew, set it off by punching a Five Percenter, without giving advance notice to any of us in the Hollis Crew. The Five Percenter (named Allah), pulled out a pistol.

Everyone scattered. Allah dropped the gun. I was one of the last ones to run out of the way. He picked the gun up and fired, hitting me in my left leg and damaging a nerve connected to my foot. I fell down, tried to get up, but fell again. I was down but Jay got to me and asked if I was hit. I said, "Yeah." So, he grabbed me by my jacket and dragged me into a classroom. I made it through that ordeal but was out of commission for quite a while, and had to re-learn how to walk.

Maybe God Had a Plan

There are quite a few other times when I've had close calls and although I grew up in a place that is known as a hotbed for many success stories, that isn't always how things turn out. A lot of guys I knew when I was growing up are either dead or doing some hard jail time. Some have escaped the treachery of the street while others are struggling; some with heroin addiction and some with financial and/or domestic drama.

Some people I know from Hollis have mellowed with age and weathered the storms of life. I am sincerely happy for them. Yet, I can't speak for anybody else. I'm best with telling my story. I've done a lot of dirt but thankfully, I've never done any real jail time. I guess I was just lucky, or maybe God had a plan for me.

Tips from a Hip Hop Vet

Taking stock of the things I've seen, done and have been exposed to, and the places I've been since starting to work professionally in hip hop, at the age of 16, it's clear that since I put in over thirty years, and I'm still heavily involved, I'm a hip hop veteran. I've learned many things from my (inside, looking out) bird's eye view. Now, for the first time, I'd like to share some of what I've learned (from my personal perspective) in book form.

Usually, I'm laid back, soaking it all up, all the while keeping my finger to the pulse. Yet the more I think about it, the more I know what happened in my life should be shared in such a way to benefit others. For example, after I got shot, I had to re-learn walking. Isn't that true with other life experiences? Sometimes we have to go back to the drawing board and re-learn something we previously knew.

Your Dreams Can Come True, Too

You may have some things you need to re-learn. If you find that to be true, don't be discouraged. This book will help you, by gently nudging you along. And this book is for anyone who has experienced setbacks in life. I've had my share of those, too. Yet, there was always a sense of something inside of me, pushing me forward. And despite the obstacles I was facing, my dreams came true and this book is all about the fact that yes, it happened for me but just as importantly, yours can, too.

There were a lot of people who I grew up with back in the day, in Hollis, and some of them traveled up and down the very same streets and similar paths that I traveled. Some went to the same schools, block parties and house parties I went to. They had similar opportunities. But that doesn't mean they were able to get their dreams to come true. That's not a criticism, just a fact. I said that to say, there are some things you must do to make it happen. Things you can do to increase your likelihood for success. I will share some of that with you, based on some things I had done.

Are You Ready?

This book is for anyone who has dreams and wants to hear from someone whose dreams have taken him around the world. This was *after* I got shot. I had to persevere, rehab, build back up my DJing skills, stay out of trouble and stay off the streets. And when my opportunity came, I was ready.

What do *you* need to do to get ready? Before we get into that, I want to take you on a quick journey into my world from where things began because you might be able to relate in some ways. I want you to get to know me a little bit. That way you could see I know what I'm talking about. Some of the places I had been in life helped me become the young man I was and the man that I am today.

Walk With Me

As I walk you through where and how it all began for me, and share with you a glimpse of how things took shape, I hope to sharpen your focus so you can see some things that you need to do in your life and situation to make your dreams come true.

If you made some wrong decisions in your life, no worries – I have, too. Determine to make things right, change your life and head down the right path. But before we go forward, come with me as I take a quick look back.

CHAPTER ONE

With a Last Name Like Fite

I always liked to fight, in P.S. 134, the elementary public school I attended while growing up in Hollis, Queens. I remember some older guys from the local junior high school, JHS 192, always coming to our schools and starting fights. One day, one of them punched me in the chest. I proceeded to whip his ass.

Once I won and started getting a reputation for being a good fighter, it felt good. Other people started to brag about me. It fed my ego, and then fighting became a regular part of my life. Plus, I am the youngest of a relatively large family. I guess somewhere along the lines, bravado kicked in because I knew my family would have my back so I was fearless

Hurricane

One day my brother, some friends and I decided we needed rap names 'cause we were getting into the rap game. I chose the name Hurricane 'cause I used to tear shit up, as a kid – toys and all. We wrote our names on my garage. I guess that kind of sealed the deal and made it official and I kind of went through life like a hurricane.

Like most kids growing up back in the 70's, I enjoyed watching karate movies. I even broke my hand, trying to chop a piece of wood in half, following something I had seen from the karate movie, "Five Fingers of Death." That was at an innocent stage of my young life but that didn't last too long because things went from hand-to-hand combat to exposure to weapons.

Some Rough Stuff

The first time I ever saw a gun, my friend Tiny (who gave himself the rap name "Butterfly") showed me his brother's .22-caliber pistol. I held it in my hand and gave it back. A short time after that, Tiny was playing with the gun and shot himself in the head. I didn't care to touch a gun for a while after that. He was a very close friend. So I stuck to fighting. But I wasn't the only one.

A friend of mine named Shelton lived across the street. He was a kid with some mental problems. One day we were playing football at the park and a guy named Sid Barnett was messing with Shelton. Shelton grabbed Sid and slammed him to the ground and pulled his ears until they were bleeding, then bit one off and spit it out. I was in shock, like "Oh shit!" There was no more football that day, just a short but long walk back to the block.

DMC

That left an impression on me as a youngster, but it didn't dissuade me from fighting. And, I didn't only fight with my fists. I constantly went to battle and proved myself on the basketball court. For a long time, DMC (Darryl McDaniels of RunDMC) wouldn't get on the mic because at the time, he thought I had more skills than him because I could rap over break beats such as Funky Drummer, Funky Penguin and Substitution. In all reality, DMC looked up to me because I was good at basketball.

I used to score 30 points or more in almost every game we played in the neighborhood parks. But on the flipside, I would be asking D to kick a rhyme he had said before, and we had mutual respect for one another.

As a matter of fact, when I got shot back when I was in high school, people would go up to DMC when he was playing the Space Invaders video game, thinking it was me – but it wasn't. I was still in the hospital rehabbing, just laying low. People also thought we were related.

Party Over Here

Through my younger years, I fought a lot but at the same time, something else was brewing in NYC and had reached our Hollis community that was also vying for my attention - hip hop. At an early age, love for music got a hold of me. I think it was partly because our house was the party house. We had parties all the time and my sister Pat (also known NYPD for New York Pat and Dee Dee, her boyfriend) was a DJ and she taught me how to scratch.

In the summertime, we'd go to block parties. And at the time, "Love Is the Message" was wafting through the air. Another tune that rocked the party right was "Trans Europe Express" by Kraftwerk, a 70's electric music group. I would hang out going to the block parties, Jamaica Avenue, Harlem and other fun romps. I mainly ran with my buddy who I hung with through elementary, junior high school and high school years – my brother from another mother, Jam Master Jay.

Jam Master Jay

Jam Master Jay and I had gotten really close in junior high school, then we went onto Andrew Jackson High School together, along with other friends. We had similar aspirations both of us became DJs. RunDMC took Jay on as their DJ. And I went on to DJ with the Beastie Boys.

Jam Master Jay (Jason Mizell) and I would eat at one another's house all of the time. We'd spend the night at each other's house. We were like brothers. We shared everything. If Jason had a girl, she had to have a girlfriend for me and vice-versa.

There were times when I had money and Jay was broke, and vice-versa. But we always held each other down, no matter what. I had known Jay forever, yet we never had one argument. And a lot of guys in the hood got to travel because once Jay got on with RunDMC, Jay took posses of friends from Hollis (aka Hollis Crew) out the hood and around the world. We went to Cali, Europe and many other places.

Gettin' Our "Grown Man" On

When we were young, Jay and I would go to Dapper Dan's (a bigtime clothing designer in Harlem, back in the day). And we would get custom made Gucci and Louis Vuitton suits. Then we'd go hang out at the Rooftop in Harlem. We would see notorious drug dealers, like Alpo. And they all respected us.

Jay and I got our fashion sense from the older cats. When we didn't go to Harlem to get fly gear, we'd sometimes go local, to Jamaica Avenue (also known as "the Ave"). We'd rock the leather jackets, pants, British Walkers, the latest track suits and the Stetson hats – just young cats, getting our "grown man" on. And if we couldn't find what we were looking for in Harlem or on Jamaica Avenue, we'd head on over to Delancey "D" Street, mainly to get our Cazals (extra wide designer framed glasses, with the lens out)

We'd also play lots of hoops. Jay was with the squad called Two Fifth Down. When we weren't playing hoops, we'd be into music. I actually started DJing before Jay. So, I would school him on the fine art of breakbeat hunting, plus a few other techniques I had learned from Davy D, who went on to become Kurtis Blow's DJ.

Davy D

Davy D, David Reeves, better known as Davy DMX was the first dope DJ in Hollis, Queens. The DMX from Davy's name is derived from the vintage Oberheim drum machine used by artists such as Prince, to lay drum tracks in the early 80's.

Davy D and I formed a group called Solo Sounds and we rocked many Hollis parties in the late 70s and early 80s. One of the first Def Jam singles, when it was an independent record label, was "Bring It," featuring Davy D, me and some ad libs by Def Jam founder, Russell Simmons.

Davy D wrote and produced Kurtis Blow's "If I Ruled the World" as well as his own hit single, "One for the Treble," and along with Larry Smith provided music for RunDMC's first two albums. Davy started off as Kurtis Blow's DJ and has worked with everyone from the legendary

LovebugStarski to Spoonie Gee and is currently a band member on Public Enemy (PE) tours. He's been around the world but it all started in Hollis.

CHAPTER TWO

Hollis, Queens

At first glance, Hollis, Queens of the 60's and 70's looked like a relatively quiet, highly respectable residential neighborhood, and it was. Famous billionaire, real estate developer and casino magnate, Donald Trump's dad (Frederick Trump) developed some of his first houses in Hollis, Queens.

Hollis has quite an impressive list of notable residents who lived there (or close by) at one time or another: Russell Simmons, Rev. Run, DMC, their DJ, Jam Master Jay, Daymond John (and all the guys from FUBU), ESPN Sports Personality Stephen A. Smith, NBA Pro Baller, Royal Ivy, LL Cool Jay (St. Albans), Ed Lover, Davy D, the 45 King, Congressman Gregory Meeks, JaRule, a Tribe Called Quest, Civil Rights Activist, Al Sharpton and "the Godfather of Soul," James Brown (St. Albans). Other Queens residents of note: Salt 'N Pepa, Kid 'N Play, Nas, 50 Cents, Roxanne Shante (Queensbridge), Young MC, the Lost Boys and many others.

Queens, Not Always What It Seems

During the 60's, when my family moved to Hollis, it was inhabited by some progressive working class black families that managed to escape some of the urban blight of the overcrowded inner cities. Things seemed to be a bit more relaxed and comfortable, and to some degree, it was. Yet, Queens can be deceptive and tends to be an underestimated borough, so don't be fooled.

As in larger society, so was Hollis: in the midst of transition. One of the things that began creeping up is something known as "white flight." Once blacks started moving up the socio-economic ladder and once we started moving into better neighborhoods, whites started moving out. Those were some heated times, between the races and we weren't co-mingling like we've become a bit better at since then. We still have a ways to go but things, in some ways, seem to be getting better.

Hollis Avenue

Back then, we had nice lawns and backyards in Hollis. Detached multi-level (mainly one or two floor single family) homes with a basement and an attic filled the residential landscape of Hollis, Queens. To help boost the local economy, a main street (Hollis Avenue) ran through Hollis which housed various businesses – a local supermarket, a pizza parlor, hair salon, barber shop, funeral home, insurance companies, a bike shop, convenience stores and other types of businesses that made the quality of life a bit better in the local area.

There was a White Castles at the corner of Hollis Avenue and Francis Lewis Boulevard. With "white flight," and an uptick in criminal behavior, it wasn't long before some of those businesses left Hollis Avenue. White Castles was no exception. It was there one day and gone the next. Still, Hollis, Queens was like a dream to some, a sign of progress for some blacks who had moved north from the south, in search of freedom from racism and Jim Crow laws that plagued the south and good job opportunities which were said to be plentiful in the north. And it was true. In many instances, things were good but in some instances, not so much. Everybody wasn't earning bucks by legitimate means.

Survival of the Fittest

The crime element that had hit Harlem (drugs and number running, to name a few things) that some believe was designed to quell the Black Power Movement, spread out to the other areas of the city where blacks were thriving, as well. Not only was organized crime running rampant throughout the city among the Italians, Irish and Chinese, but levels of semi-organized crime hit Hollis, too. Drug infestation, gun smuggling and other elements of ill-repute also hit the Hollis streets in the 1960s and 70s. Gangs such as the Seven Crowns, the Seven Immortals and Savage Skulls terrorized some individuals, streets and schools.

What was happening on the adult level had trickled down to the kiddie level so robberies started becoming commonplace. Kids were being picked on. Or they decided not to be victimized, so they picked on other kids. A simple trip to the grocery store might mean your mom's milk and bread money got taken. It was "survival of the fittest." If you went to the basketball court, you might get your basketball taken. If you rode your bike, you didn't want to ride alone. You might get jacked for your bike.

Beefs

On top of local infighting, other parts of Queens like South Jamaica (often referred to as "Southside" where the infamous "40 Projects" are), Queensbridge and even parts of Brooklyn (aptly referred to as Crooklyn, because of high crime in some parts) would hate on us. Sometimes, it was clashes because of jealousy. Some kids didn't like the fact that we seemed to have it so good, living in houses when they lived in the projects. A true case of the "haves" and the "have nots." So we'd have beef not just between boroughs but between different parts of the same borough. Like Queensbridge and Southside would come at Hollis, in Queens. And we'd go after them.

What were we going to do? Stay in the house? No, we still dared to venture outside, have fun and try to make the most of things. We'd go to the parks and we'd go to the pool. The Liberty Park Pool wasn't in Hollis but it was close enough for us to walk to Liberty Avenue (or at least take the Q2 bus most of the way) and go to the Liberty Park Pool.

Hip Hop: to the Rescue

I remember a bunch of us went swimming, one time. We were playing and I fell in the deep part of the pool. I couldn't swim and almost drowned. An Asian man saved my life. I never went swimming again. After that, I stayed local, most of the time - in Hollis. Hip hop was just coming on the scene. So I dabbled in it, as a hobby. We would go to house parties, block parties and jams at Junior High School 192 and Jamaica Park - just having fun as kids.

Neighborhood music heroes were coming to the forefront, like Master Sounds (Ed Lover). The crew I was in with Davy D (before he got scooped up by Kurtis Blow, to be his DJ, Solo Sounds, was known all over. Playgrounds, block parties and house parties became stages and performances that had us kids rushing home to practice so the next day or week we could come back better, stronger, more original and more clever than our peers.

B-Ballin' and Yes Y'allin'

Playgrounds and parks ceased being such violent places and gave way to creativity. Literal stars were born at JHS 192's playground and at Jamaica Park. Week after week and year after year, we'd battle one another, just for fun. We used to not only battle one another in rap but we battled one another in basketball.

I was a very good basketball player as a kid. There was a part of Hollis known as 205th Down. I was so good at ball, once I dropped over 60 points on 205thDown. In sports, they had Greg Smith, Jeff Fludd and Fat Fludd, to name a few. And these are some of the same guys who did major things once hip hop blew up. Jeff Fludd, at the age of 19, was RunDMC's manager.

Drugs, Staying Fresh....

Yet the drug element was always lurking nearby. Hollis, Queens is very close to the start of Long Island (Nassau County). So once the drugs started flowing through Hollis streets, some kids from Long Island would no longer have to travel to Harlem or Manhattan to get drugs. They'd come to Hollis and other parts of Queens that were dealing drugs. The guys who were making moves in the streets were hometown heroes. Especially in homes where there was an absence of a fathers. The guys who were making quick and large sums of money, dressing nicely and mingling with pretty women appealed to me.

I looked up to the older guys in my 'hood and older OG's (the street elders – derived from the term Original Gangsta, although the person doesn't necessarily have to be gang-affiliated), like Biggie Owen, who lived on Francis Lewis Boulevard, was like a father-figure to me. He was one of the first number runners in Hollis, and he stayed fly. So, we copied them, on our level. We'd rock Adidas, Pumas, British Walkers, Lee Jeans, the girls wore Jordache. And we also sported big gold and Cazals (designer eyeglasses, often with the lenses out, just for fashion – as some wear geek glasses now, to look smart).

...And More Drugs

There was a also guy named Chili Lee from Hollis that saw how much money was being made by a drug spot on Hollis Avenue called Sunnyside. He also saw how much traffic was flowing into and out of Sunnyside and he wanted to flourish like that. So, Chili Lee went to Harlem, bought some angel dust, teamed with his friend, King Allah, and they started making a fortune, selling dust.

As a kid, I started following suit. I started selling it and smoking it. How I did not end up drug addicted is a wonder. My first time trying cocaine, I was on my way, walking to school (Andrew Jackson High School, which although it's in Cambria Heights is right next to Hollis, Queens).

I was a freshman and Kurtis Blow was in a car sitting in the front of my school, just posted up, waiting for me. He saw me, called my name and told me to get in the car. I got in and he passed me a bill with coke in it. I was impressed with this guy and didn't want to disappoint him, so I took some hits and into *high* school I went, HIGH.

CHAPTER THREE

Andrew Jackson

The guy on the $20-bill, the 7th president of the United States of America, Andrew Jackson, would turn over in his grave if he knew about things that were happening in the Cambria Heights high school named after him when I went there - but then again, maybe not.

Andrew Jackson was a colonel and major general in the United States Army during the Revolutionary War, Creek War, the War of 1812 and the First Seminole War (which resulted in the conquest of Florida). People better watch what they name schools. Good thing Andrew Jackson High School was renamed.

"Old Hickory," as Andrew Jackson was referred to, was known for his toughness and aggressive personality. There were plenty of people like that in attendance at Jackson when I went. But, on the good side of things, the basketball team (with the school's green and white colors and Bulldogs team mascot), went by the name of the Hickories.

Coach Chuck Granby

After four and a half decades, at the age of 79, Coach Chuck Granby recently retired from coaching Andrew Jackson's hoop squad. With 722 wins, 24 division titles and 7 borough titles, Coach Granby is a living legend – having the most victories in the history of New York's Public School Athletic League. Granby is such a winner, he beat cancer twice. In 1976, Granby fought and beat cancer in his kidney and in 1993, he got the victory over cancer in his prostate gland. Good thing because many lives have been affected.

Granby was a father figure to many of his players from broken homes. Granby's impeccable reputation remained even in the midst of the drugs, violence and low achievement often associated with Andrew Jackson High School. Granby hung in there in the midst of all the fights, demonstrations and turmoil. He continued to forge ahead and he did so with such poise. He lived an exemplary life before his players. A clear indication of that is: in all those years, Granby *never* received a technical foul during any of the games he coached.

Some of the standout players under Granby's tutelage include Lloyd Daniels, Derrick Hawkins "Hawk," Tyrone "Bo" Edwards, Kyle O'Quinn who plays for the Orlando Magic and Greg "Boo" Harvey who averaged 38 points per game in his senior year and had the standing record for 10 years (which cannot be broken due to Jackson officially closing in 1994, and being renamed Campus Magnet High School) of 2,039 points. Boo's son, Justin, followed in his dad's footsteps by being coached by Granby. Boo went onto to shine at St. John's University. These are just a few of the dynamic players graced with the privilege of playing for Coach Granby.

From 1972 – 1985, the Hickories did not lose a home game. What a bright shining light in the midst of all the bad press Jackson was getting, as being one of the worse schools in New York City. And we won't even get into the sassy, sexy and soulful syncopation that the cheerleaders displayed at the games.

What had happened to the school attended by ABC's hit TV series, "Scandal's," Papa Pope (Joe Morton) and basketball luminary and racial equality advocate, Bob Cousy?

Lurking in the Shadows

That was the bright side, on the dark side: what was happening in the society made its way into the school. Drugs had so tightly gripped it so badly, that in 1970, police broke up a heroin-processing factory in Andrew Jackson High School's basement.

When I went to Jackson, you could get robbed at 8 am. Thankfully, we had older Hollis guys in the school already, like Kool E – who was respected. But once we got in there, shit got tough. We had beef with the Five Percent Nation. It was all out-war. The Five Percent Nation had members from all over. A lot of them used to join the Nation for protection.

In the Jackson lunchrooms, Hollis Crew had big dice games, like we had in Hollis. The school spilled over with activities that took place in the community.

Southside vs. the Hollis Crew

One time a guy from Southside Jamaica said he wanted to fight one of our friend's named "White Boy Kev." One Hollis Crew member threw a big garbage can over his head. Then everybody started to whip his ass. They had to wheel him out in a wheelchair.

The Hollis Crew ran the school when I attended. Southside was outnumbered. There were times when the police detectives walked the halls, looking for suspects they wanted. My friend, "Big O," went to jail, catching a 1-to-3 year sentence, for knocking out a security guard.

The school hired a task force to get rid of us. We were just "off tha' chain," (reckless). I don't blame them. As things turned out, our house in Hollis went up in flames, so my family relocated to Corona, Queens – to live with my stepfather who had a huge house. We went from living in a two-bedroom (with six of us) to a 6-bedroom house. Andrew Jackson found out about my new address and kicked me out, making me go to Flushing High School.

When I left Jackson, Jason (Jam Master Jay) was one of the last guys from Hollis left. The Jackson administration did not remove the guys from the Five Percent Nation. So, they moved on Jay - one of them sucker-punched Jason. He was outnumbered so he couldn't do much, but he called me.

Right away, I had to go up there and handle that situation. After all, I had a beef in Flushing High School two days earlier and Jay had come up there for me, to help make sure we had a fair, one-on-one fight where no one jumped in. Gone are those days!

I whipped the guy's ass. So the next day, Hollis Crew got together to support Jay and we rolled up to the school, like 50 strong. We walked in the school from all angles. In the melee, I ended up getting shot. After I got shot, it was an all-out war against the Nation of Five Percenters, every day.

I wasn't in the midst of those battles because I was recuperating and being rehabilitated. Jay would come by and visit me a lot. You would think after such an experience I had learned my lesson and would give up such foolishness. But I didn't. It took a while.

I'm glad the former Andrew Jackson High School, now named Campus Magnet High School, is doing much better now than it was when I was going there. They have relevant courses for these days and times, such as: community service, political science, technology, business and entrepreneurship.

And even before Jackson became new and improved, some other well-known celebrities attended: LL Cool J and 50 Cents. And there are countless numbers of Andrew Jackson High School graduates who have proceeded from Jackson to enter into all fields of the working, citizen and domestic spectrum. But I cannot erase what happened to me there and some of what lingered in the aftermath.

CHAPTER FOUR

Stick 'Em Up

I had been convalescing in Corona, Queens. My plans were to get my education, make music and play ball again, but that notion got thrown out of the window when (shortly after I had gotten back on my feet), some guys on Northern Boulevard pulled out guns and robbed me of my gold chain. Before that, I would never carry a gun (remembering what happened to my childhood buddy, Tiny) but after I had gotten robbed at gunpoint, I wouldn't be caught without one. I had met some Puerto Ricans and Dominicans, in the area, who gave me some guns.

I would get some Hollis guys to come to Corona and rob the guys who robbed me. That went on for at least two months straight. At the same time, the war was still on with the Five Percent Nation. I was traveling back and forth between Corona and my old, Hollis 'hood.

Sincerely Wrong

One day, we (from the Hollis Crew) were on the train. We were about 40 deep. A big dude named Sincere was on the train. He had two others with him. When the doors to the train opened at 169th Street, our friend Dave Seabrook (who later married Sammy "the Bull" Gravano's daughter), robbed Sincere of some Cazal shades.

Sincere grabbed the train door, to keep it from closing. My man Kule June put a pistol to Sincere's face, then he let the doors close. We got off at the next exit. Ten cop cars pulled up. Sincere had told on us. We passed the guns to some girls that were with us. Luckily, the cops didn't search the girls, but they arrested Jay, Big O, Dave, Kim Washington, White Girl Laurie, Kule June and Box Head. Because there were so many of us, some of us managed to get away without incident. Was that enough to stop me from participating in the street madness? Not really.

A Different Train Caper

Another time, I was on the train with my brother, Kule June and a guy named Chuckie. We were hanging with some girls from Long Island when we got into an altercation with the guy on the train. I grabbed the guy and threw him into the window of the train, but I pulled him back before he fell all the way out of the window. Automatically, the train stopped.

As soon as we got off the train, a bunch of police were swarming. To make matters worse, the guy I had been fighting lied to the cops and said I robbed him, claiming the ring I was sporting was his. Not so, it was Jam Master Jay's. Just so happens we all took pictures before we had gotten on the train. I had the ring on *before* I got on the train.

I told Jay what happened and of course he had to go to court to testify that the ring was his. But before we could go all the way with the court case, the guy folded because we gave him "that look" (mean mugging him) – and he was "shook" and refused to go forward with the case.

Seems like I was always doing some dirt with Kule June, he was my stick up partner. We would rob folks in a heartbeat. We wouldn't kill anybody or anything like that but people definitely had to "run them pockets" (turn over whatever valuables were stashed in pockets – and pocketbooks) We'd do crazy things for money, putting ourselves in all kinds of danger.

Do Tha' Hustle

To get money, we used to go to "the city" (Manhattan) and buy something called "Coco Snow" (fake cocaine). When we got back "around the way" (Hollis), we would sell the fake cocaine to people who came to our area looking for a quick high. Right after we made a few quick sales, my crew and I would leave the scene immediately after the transactions – just in case a dissatisfied customer came back wanting their money.

We did that a few times with not just coke, but also hash. The people who bought the fake drugs thought they were getting weed until they smoked it. But that hustle did not last long. We just did it a couple of times (to get some fast cash) until we got enough money to get our hands on some real shit. Eventually, those interests faded and I just concentrated on doing what I was supposed to be doing.

Making Things Better

When I was recovering from getting shot, I rehabbed at home in Corona, lifting weights and I got back to practicing on the turntables. It got to a certain point that no one had seen me for almost a year, except Jason and a few others from Hollis that came to visit me.

I was a skinny kid but I packed a good punch. I had a cousin who lived next door and he was a workout beast. I followed his workout, rehabbing my foot back from nerve damage. It was so bad, I couldn't raise my foot up for a while and I worked until I was able to get it raised. My big toe, to this day, does not come all the way up but I worked hard and got back most of my feelings and I started back to playing lots of ball after I got better.

How We Doin' It – Now

My younger years of being a stick up kid are long in my rear view mirror of life. Those petty crimes were not major, on the grand scale of things. I rapped about it because I was in it, to a degree and I was around it. I have since moved on and have found way less dangerous ways to have adventures and get money – legitimate ways.

With the advent of technology, I am realizing the potential to reach more people than I did back when I was on tour with the Beastie Boys or being a bodyguard for RunDMC. I am in the process of remixing what I know and bringing it up to speed in the technological age. Plenty of people around the world are just becoming aware of things we used to do decades ago. I'm willing to share the knowledge.

Don't Sleep

A lot of times, DJs don't get their due (respect, money, etc.) But life has a funny way of bringing things around full circle. I honestly believe I was short-changed in many instances, but I'm not going to gripe about it because there is plenty more in store. I have a better understanding of how to command what I am worth, and I recognize my value.

I am assembling a team and have been working on a number of projects beneath the surface. I think the biggest indication that there is more for me to do is the fact that despite all of my shenanigans, I did not become a statistic.

CHAPTER FIVE

Not a Statistic

That I'm alive today is not something I take for granted. Whenever I go up and down the Hollis streets where I grew up, I am always reminded of the people I knew who died. There are so many who have died on Hollis streets that if a tombstone were to be placed where each of those people have died, it would look like a cemetery. But, I am so glad I'm not a statistic.

I marvel when I look at stats because I could have easily been one of them. A set of Bureau of Justice statistics from 2007 showed that there were about 8,000 reported homicides in the United States. An alarming stat that jumped out at me is that 93% of the people who were murdered were killed by people of the same race.

Crazy Numbers

So black folks, we can't say, "It's the white folks killing us." Not true, we're doing it to ourselves. About 22 blacks were murdered each day by other blacks. That's crazy! And what's equally staggering is: there are somewhat similar numbers among whites. Among whites who were victims in single-victim homicides perpetrated by single-offenders, 85% of the white victims were murdered by someone of their race.

In incidences of homicide among the black race, 85% of the victims were males – and 51% were between the ages of 17-29. So, while some people are against aging, for a black guy to hit the age of 30 and beyond is a good thing. I'm all for it!

Blacks are killed with firearms in about 77% of homicides committed against them. So back when I was a kid and wrote the song, "StickEm Up," I had no idea how serious the issue really was. But not only that, another major thing that plagues a lot of people no matter where I go is fatherlessness – kids growing up without the presence of their dads in their lives.

Homes without Dads

According to census data, since I've been born (around 50 years ago), the number of children living in a single-parent household throughout the United States has nearly doubled. In 2010, *twenty million* children were living in homes without one parent. As a result of such a vacancy in the father department, many children become victims of street life because of following the males who are out and about doing what they do in the streets.

There are higher rates of juvenile delinquents in homes where the father is absent. There tends to be higher numbers of children with behaviour problems because they have no father at home to answer to. Not always, but children who grow up with no dad at home tend to end up in poverty.

Marriage Matters Financially

When the economy is working okay, married couples bring in about $80,000 to their homes each year. It's a whole other thing in single-parent households, and these homes usually have more than one kid. On average, a single person brings in about $24,000 to their household every year.

In black homes throughout the nation, 54% of children are being raised by single mothers. So you know what the deal is for them money-wise. It's not a pretty picture. So, the spiral continues downward into crime because of jacked-up financial situations at home. That leads to high numbers of incarcerations, particularly for black males.

Dark Spike in Prison Population

According to an NAACP Criminal Justice Fact Sheet, from 1980-2008 the number of people incarcerated in America *quadrupled* from around 500,000 to 2.3 million people. Out of that 2.3 million people, nearly a million of them are African-Americans.

Unfortunately, for some, prison is like a revolving door. Sometimes, people seem to do better in prison, (having three squares [square meals] and a cot [a place to sleep]) than in their own home. So some guys would rather take a chance on a life of crime because they think they don't have (m)any options.

Things Are Working Out

Make no mistake about it. I could have easily been a dude who did some real time in prison but somehow things worked out in a way that it didn't happen to me. And I'm no longer doing the crazy things I was doing when I was a kid. That's a good thing. And in a sense, I was a statistic for a while (with no father in our home), but that changed. And I became determined to not let that be the situation my kids had to face.

I am very involved in my children's lives, and I am happy to be that way. I know what it feels like to be without a dad at key moments in your life. I didn't want to cause my children that pain. So, I'm there for them as much as I can be. And even with that, there's still more ground to cover because I still have things to accomplish in life and I am still fighting my way through.

CHAPTER SIX

Still Fighting My Way Through

Many people thought hip hop was going to die, or that it's dead but nothing could be further from the truth. Hip hop is here and it's not going anywhere. Hip hop is worldwide. Yet as vast as hip hop is: I still find myself fighting my way through, to continue making a living in the culture I love.

Transitions

Hip hop has gone through numerous transitions since it was birthed when I was a kid. It went from being NY-based to spreading throughout the country before going around the world. Even before that, it had to be accepted and embraced.

Initially, hip hop was thought to be thuggish, and exclusive to young black kids. But music is universal and hip hop became embraced by white kids, then finally celebrated by other cultures and generations. Now, hip hop is somewhat mainstream. It's everywhere.

It's unfortunate, though, because it's happened repeatedly with music in the black culture. It's minimized when blacks are the only ones doing it, but once the scope broadens the acceptance is there and it seems like the blacks get squeezed out and others benefit. So much of that has happened in hip hop.

Deals (and big bucks) are made. But what happens to the pioneers and the trailblazers? I've seen far too many fall by the wayside and end up penniless. I am not blaming anybody, just making some observations. And to add to that, it's on individuals to take personal responsibility for their lives, careers and the business associated with it.

In the words of the late, great poet laureate Maya Angelou, "When you know better, you should do better." And that is what I am in the midst of doing and discovering as it pertains to hip hop.

Re-Inventing Myself

As a grown man, I'm not the kid I was who toured overseas and throughout the country as a bodyguard for RunDMC (back in the eighties) and the guy who was DJ for the Beastie Boys for over a decade. Even though I've been grown and a family man for quite a while, I still have a heart that beats hip hop. So, what I've had to do to make myself relevant as hip hop has gone through its various phases is: contemporize and re-invent myself.

My finger is still to the pulse of hip hop. And I can't even front, with all of the technology and social media, it's hard to keep up with all that's going on in the hip hop world now. And it's okay. I don't have to do it all.

The main thing I need to do now is remain active. To that end, I went from being a consumer of hip hop and a pioneering contributor to the culture – and I am now at the point of molding and shaping the career of another artist, and others will come along. In addition, I share information of my experiences on the college level. I've been a guest lecturer on college campuses, and am slating similar opportunities for the future.

Relevance

One of the main things in hip hop, as I get older, (and I'm sure it's true in many other areas of life), is maintaining relevance. Really, it's somewhat of a struggle. But then it's not all that difficult. Having kids of my own keeps me aware of what's going on with the younger generation. And I keep myself informed by not only reading about what's going on, but I literally stay in the mix. I still DJ. I attend conferences. I speak at conferences and I do instructional videos.

Hip hop is far from dead. There's so much ground to cover. I'm actually finding it tough to keep up with (and bring about) all of the ideas I have that keep coming to me. As I constantly make plans to move forward, I pause for a moment and gladly reflect on the fact that I have beaten the odds.

CHAPTER SEVEN

Beating the Odds

Many times people try to do things that never happen. I am not patting myself on the back but I am acknowledging my successes that in some instances may seem small but they really matter because they are stepping stones not only in taking me from where I was to where I was going, but they serve as the building blocks I refer to as I help guide others into their successes also.

I Became a DJ

It might not seem like a big deal to some people but I did something at such a young age that grown-ups are to this day trying to do. Not so much the DJ part, but the part where I became a *paid* DJ – where I did (and do) it for a living. Who does that? Get paid to do what you love doing....

Not bragging, but I did it and so can you. Sure, growing up in Hollis and having a sister with DJ equipment lent itself to my success in a big way, but I firmly believe that it really doesn't matter. If you have something in your heart to do, and you move in that direction, things will open up for you. The resources and instruction you need will be there for you.

Will it happen like, poof, one day you want to be something and the next day you're that thing. No, you have to apply yourself and chase down whatever it is you want to do and be in life. As I reflect, I think of the many kids growing up in Hollis back in the day. I'm sure there are others who may have wanted to be a DJ. Some did it, and some didn't. What made the difference in me doing it and them not doing it? There are a lot of factors: some of it was pure luck, passion, preparation and persistence.

Preparation

Of the four things I just mentioned that helped me to have my dreams come true, two of them I can't really speak on because with luck, I can't say how something like that happens. And regarding passion, if it's not there it's just not there. But, I could talk about preparation and persistence. That's something I definitely was able to play a part in, paving the way for my dreams coming true.

I didn't know it at the time but I was preparing for my success by becoming aware of what the good music was, the break parts, on the records. That took some time. I spent many hours sifting through records, listening to them, over and over again until I got sounds I could put together and get a party rocking right.

I observed a lot, too. I didn't just jump out there and get to DJ. For a good while I watched. I became a student of the process. I didn't just lay in the cut, and let it go over my head. I paid attention. I got up on what I wanted to do, up close and it became personal. And then I persistently pursued my passion.

Persistence

I am not some overnight sensation. I stayed at it, minute after minute, hour after hour, day after day, week after week, month after month and year after year. And I'm still here. I think those early days, and putting in all of that time helps in my longevity.

Yes, it was fun going around from party to party and going around to the different clubs. But after a while, that wears thin. If there wasn't a persistence in me, to keep going, and doing what I needed to do to get on the wheels of steel and make something happen, I wouldn't have become a part of the crew. I would have just faded into oblivion and been a part of the crowd.

Nothing wrong with being part of the crowd, enjoying the parties, clubs and chilling but if you want to see your dreams become a reality, you have to stretch beyond what everybody else is doing and you have to persist. You have to keep at it until you get what you want and you're doing what you want to do.

Turning My Life Around

Another key factor in me being able to have my dreams come true was I turned my life around. The streets were there, and they're still there. What changed? Me. I had to come to the point where I did less and less of what I knew I shouldn't be doing and more and more of what I should be doing.

I focused on my education. I got my GED. I got inside myself and decided I wanted to do something with my life, and I had a good opportunity before me. I was basically a reserved dude, and I had my times of joking around but I kind of got serious and as a result, I've been able to avoid a disastrous outcome.

Sometimes you've got to walk away from destructive things and people. I've lived long enough to see what happens to people who continue on a self-defeating path and really it boils down to choices. I *chose* to turn my life around. And if you know, deep down in your heart you're heading in the wrong direction, I suggest you do the same so you can beat the odds, too.

I think about all the times I had the ability to get out of sticky situations. Time after time after time, I was in the midst of people who either got into trouble, went to jail or some of my peers have been murdered. Yet I'm still here and I figure there must be a reason.

CHAPTER EIGHT

There Must Be a Reason

Being able to live my life and do what I love to do has been (and is) fun. It's very fulfilling. I get to do music, travel the world and meet great people. Who wouldn't love to do that? It's exciting, it's uplifting and there's still an element of challenge that goes into it but there's more.

Experience

I'm not a rookie. I'm not some new jack on the scene. I've been at it for a while, decades. I've gained quite a bit of valuable experience through the years, through my activities and based on the people and situations I've encountered throughout the music and hip hop world. Along the way, I've received guidance regarding what to do, what not to do, what to say and what not to say.

My eyewitness experience has helped me learn the ropes and come to my own conclusions, based on what I've seen and heard plus based on what the elders in the field have taught me. I'm now at the point where others seek me out for advice. I've been poised to give advice for a while now. It's just becoming more and more clear to me that it's now time for me to take an active role in helping others based on my experience.

I am able to skilfully give others things to consider when they embark on the journey of becoming a DJ or a hip hop artist. Where some people are trying to get to, I've already been. Some things people are trying to learn, I've forgotten and learned some new things. Sometimes nothing is more valuable than getting insight from someone who has been where you're trying to go. Seek out people who have "been there and done that."

Each One Teach One

You have to humble yourself and graciously know when it's time for you to get out of the spot light and prep someone else so they can get their shine one. It's not always easy. You get a sense of sadness and wonder if you still have what it takes. Yes, I do but I also have sense enough to know when it's time to impart my knowledge to the next generation.

It doesn't have to be anything deep, just share what you know. It's a type of selflessness where you remember all the people who took the time to show you what you know, and you do the same thing for someone else.

There's something so rewarding in sharing information with someone who, yes, they knew some things but when I shared what I knew it added to what they know. And sometimes, it's not for anything but for the love of what I do. In some instances, it's just the spark someone needs to keep them going in a positive direction.

I am now to the point where I teach on various levels but not everybody is going to do that. Start where you are. Just remember this: the most celebrated DJ and/or hip hop artist, or whoever is at the top of your chosen field was once a beginner at some point. Someone taught them. You'll never know who you have in your midst. And if you have a willing student, and you have the ability to teach them what you know, why not give them a shot?

Not Living My Life in Vain

Sometimes people go through life and they don't amount to much - seems like they're just taking up space. After the years kept rolling on, I made the determination that I would not live my life in vain. I want it to be meaningful to not just myself but to others. Yes, I could make them feel good by rocking a party right but what if they go home and they don't have any food in their pantry.

I know what it's like to be low on funds. I think part of my job since I've been spared my life and given opportunity after opportunity is to help others. Am I able to save the world? No, that's not what I was put here on Earth to do. Matter of fact, I'm still grappling with things myself. But I can encourage people, helping them in different ways. Plus, I can try to make this a better place and I think I started to get an inkling of this when I got my inspiration to actually wholeheartedly embrace this thing called hip hop.

CHAPTER NINE

I Can Do This Thing Called Hip Hop

When I was a kid, I did not realize it then but I was in the midst of a groundbreaking musical revolution. Hint: you never know, you might be in the midst of some type of groundbreaking revolution yourself. But, can you imagine.... I was in elementary school with the late great Jam Master Jay. Who knew that he'd become; what he became?

Russell Simmons was a party promoter, just trying to cause people to have a good time. He was making money by pushing parties. Who knew that he'd become?

It was just like jumping in a pool for me, and swimming around. I got right in where I fit in and was having fun. All the while I was honing skills because I was doing this on a daily basis. I was going hard. Each day brought new adventures and new, creative and competitive battles. I didn't want to get chumped so, I figured how to be good at it.

Some of the older cats saw a legitimate way to make money off of hip hop, even though it wasn't even called that back then. Other people, outside of the hip hop culture, began to capitalize as well. Show and concert promoters eventually came on the scene, as well as record executives. And even clothing marketers started showing up.

Hip hop audiences and crowds became known for their high level of materialism and consumption, an easy target for marketers. But somewhere along the lines, I became aware that there was money to be made. So, I kept at it, steadily getting better and better.

Follow Your Passion

I loved making music and seeing people have fun at parties. And I kept doing it and before long I had a marketable skill in the hip hop world. First, I started as a bodyguard. Even before I became a DJ, I just wanted to be around hip hop. So, I took a job on tour with RunDMC, as a bodyguard. I had grown tall and was pumping weights. I wasn't that little kid anymore. Last name's Fite, remember?

So, I stayed real close to hip hop. Yet, at the same time, I never lost sight of my love for making music. I kept spinning. I kept my weight up at the turntables. And others knew what I could do. And since I stayed ready, a major opportunity presented itself when I was with RunDMC (as a bodyguard) on the landmark *Raising Hell Tour*.

The Beastie Boys also had gone on tour with RunDMC, as well as LL Cool J, Whodini and a West Coast group, Timex Social Club (TSC), who had a hit song out back then called "Rumours." At one point during the tour, the original Beastie Boys' DJ, Doctor Dre, couldn't go because he had a job as host of MTV's *Yo! MTV Raps*. Guess who got the open slot to DJ? Moi!

I didn't have to get ready, I *was* ready. Not everything was perfect but I was able to successfully step in and stay on for more than a decade following that. What started as something that seemed temporary ended up being permanent for quite a while because I was doing something I loved, and getting paid to do it. And the big bonus on top of that was I got to travel some more, places I had never been before.

I was on the road, traveling to London, across the country to Cali, numerous times. We wound down that *Raising Hell Tour* playing at Madison Square Garden – oh yes indeed! I had lots of fun, did all the crazy things that young cats do. But something was missing in my life.

CHAPTER TEN

A New Dawn in My Life, My Wife

I'm considered by some to be a handsome guy. So, I never had a problem getting girls. I had watched the moves of the older guys I grew up around and learned along the way. So I knew what I needed to know about girls. And to tell the truth, that was one of the perks that went with going on tour - all of the women. Once I started getting on TV and going on tours, it got out of hand.

In the mid 1980's my childhood buddy, Jam Master Jay and I would double-date. If I had a girl, she had to have a friend for me and vice-versa. But I got burnt out from dealing with too many women. Yet, it was hard for me to fall in love with someone because I always had distractions. That all changed the Summer of 1985. It was then that I met the young lady (named Dawn) who became my wife.

We were on and off, dating a lot. I had a son and she had a daughter, both the same age. And she and I were the same age. Seemed like a perfect fit. As time went on, we got closer and closer. Then we moved in together.

I decided during a video shoot. There were "easy pickings." A bunch of girls were around me and I could have had any one (or some) of them that I wanted. But I had gotten to a point where that was not what I wanted. So, I called Dawn and asked her to marry me.

I am happy to say that my marriage has remained in tact. Yes, we have had the normal ups and downs, like any good marriage, or anything worthwhile. I am happily married and to this union we have added an additional daughter and son. And our family has branched out even further since then.

I'm not saying I'm Dr. Phil, Steve Harvey or any of those guys but since I've managed to stay married this long, I could give a bit of advice. Nothing deep but to the guys I would advise you to realize you will never win an argument. Don't waste your breath. And yelling isn't necessary because things get escalated and can turn physical at some point.

The advice I have for women is: learn not to nag about everything. Let your man have some breathing room so he doesn't feel locked down.

Is that all there is to a good marriage? Of course not, but it could help in some ways - even if just a little bit. And another thing: communication is key. Not that you'll agree on everything. If you married the clone of yourself, you might as well have stayed single. But you didn't and the sooner you realize you are two distinct people with all kinds of differences, the better off you'll be.

You might have good compatibility, but you are different from your spouse and the bridge over that gap is communication. Keep the lines of communication open, especially when you have your differences and quarrels. Oh, let me throw this in as a bonus, you don't always have to win. Dudes, if you're competing against your wife and you win, in a sense you lose because you're supposed to be on the same team.

A lot of times people venture outside of their marriage thinking, "the grass is greener on the other side" – until they get to the other side. So, if you have a good marriage, stick with it. There's work involved but it's worth it. And while I'm on that topic, let me go in a little bit deeper.

Work It Out

Some of the stuff we learn as kids, on playgrounds (conflict resolution – when it's done peacefully, respect, loyalty and honor) – are applicable to marriage situations. Anything worth striving for, obtaining and keeping for a while, is worth putting in the extra effort to make sure it remains intact. So, if you have situations and issues in your marriage that are not oppressive and abusive, I recommend you work it out – especially if there are kids involved.

Take time to figure out why you got together with your spouse in the first place. Maybe that can be the glue that holds you together for a while. Then make plans for your current situation, seeking out ways to improve and enhance your marriage. And think long-term. Plot and plan for your future. Hopefully, that will keep your marriage on track.

Children

I love my wife dearly, to the ends of the Earth – and beyond. And the bonus is our children. Children have a way of reminding you of some things you may have let slip with time. Having children caused me to re-think my purpose, or at least try to figure out why I exist. Is it all about me? Or am I concerned about their well-being?

Provision for my children and family is paramount in my life. Actually, it makes me go even harder in hip hop and my other activities because the more I have, that means the better life can be for them. And having kids helps me to constantly weigh the consequences of my actions.

When I was younger, I did dumb things without any thought. No rhyme or reason. Now, my thoughts are along the lines of: *How will what I do affect my wife, my family and my kids? What we built (and are building)....* I am one of their primary role models.

Kids don't go by what you say. They go by what you *do* and/or don't do. Hopefully, how I live my life is a good example for my kids and they want to follow in my footsteps. Not necessarily the same thing that I do but the way I conduct myself as I do what I do.

A good work ethic is major if you want your dreams to come true. This is not just for hip hop but it applies to life in general. Anybody who wants to flourish has got to put in the work.

CHAPTER ELEVEN

Putting in the Work

A lot of times people look at life on the hip hop scene and think it's easy. That's an illusion. Are there endless girls? Seems like it sometimes but that's not all there is to it. There's a whole lot of hard work involved. People get successful in the hip hop and any other industry and in their lives by putting in the work. For me, that means doing my job.

Doing My Job

Quite a while ago, I got to a point in my life when I realized "playtime is over." It was time to get serious about my future, and what I needed to do to secure a profitable future on behalf of my family and myself.

I started out as a bodyguard. And with all of those people pressing up, trying to get close to RunDMC and Jam Master Jay, I had to be on the alert and not get swooped up by all of the temptations and distractions. I had to be at my post and be on the alert.

At times, it was long nights and lots of travel – going from place to place, turning around and doing the same thing day after day. It wasn't time for me to be out partying and sightseeing. I had to maintain focus and put in work, paying my dues.

Things didn't happen for me all at once. I was doing things daily but it took a while before my hard work paid off. I took it all in stride and stayed on task by taking things one step at a time.

One Step at a Time

A lot of times, people get ahead of themselves, looking too far into the future and they skip over taking care of what's right in front of them. One of the hallmark things about hip hop is freestyle, like in rap, it's on the spur of the moment. It's unrehearsed. Life is like that. And if you don't have the temperament to easily adjust to such great change and fluctuation, it could unnerve you.

To steady my pace as I ran (and run) in the rap race, I take things one step at a time. And it's taken me far from my starting point. And I believe that method of operation will take me even further in the music and hip hop industry. Another key factor in making my dreams come true is mental toughness.

Mental Toughness

A hip hop life is not for the faint-hearted. Touring to promote albums is *not* a "walk in the park." It requires high levels of mental toughness and self-confidence. Your mind has to be right if you're going to have your dreams come true because there are so many things that happen along the way. And if your mind's not right, you could drift and get sidetracked.

Basically, you have to run over in your mind how you would like things to be. It's like a video in your mind. Think of scenarios that you have been through. Then see yourself running along the course as you hope things will be. That can help bridge the gap to get you to your dreams. And again, your need for self-confidence cannot be overemphasized.

Self-Confidence

When I speak of self-confidence, I'm not talking about you thinking about how great you are in an arrogant or conceited way. I'm speaking more along the lines of having a good healthy dose of confidence about your ability to get the job done and have the skills necessary to do what is asked of you.

It doesn't happen automatically, it comes with exercise – by doing something over and over again, and knowing what to do and what you should not do. You gain experience and that boosts your self confidence. And of course you'll need that when you're in the midst of haters.

There's always going to be some sorry person who is not happy because you're doing what you want to do and your life is good. Well, that's too bad. Hold your head up and do what you want to do. Figure out how to make your dreams come true and enjoy the satisfaction that this type of life brings.

The pinnacle of my success in the hip hop world (so far) has been when I was on tour with RunDMC and as I was the DJ for the Beastie Boys. I mentioned it a little earlier but I think it would be good to pause here and reflect about when I went *on the Raising Hell Tour* in 1986 because that tour changed everything for me.

CHAPTER TWELVE

"Raising Hell" Tour (1986)

I left Hollis to go on RunDMC'sgroundbreaking*Raising Hell* hip hop tour as a bodyguard. When that tour was over, I was a DJ for the Beastie Boys.

We had gone on the tour to promote RunDMC's 3rd album, *Raising Hell.* We did that for three months. It was a mixture of hip hop, rap and rock.

RunDMC were rising in popularity and controversy at the same time. A bunch of kids would come to the concert and if things went wrong, RunDMC were accused of being a catalyst but that's really not true. For example, in Long Beach, California, all hell really did break loose. Some gang warfare took place during a concert.

It's not the hip hop or the artists who incited the mayhem. Those gangbangers were gonna go at it whether RunDMC were there or not. They just took the opportunity to express their animosity towards one another during the concert. It was so bad that the following scheduled concert (at the Hollywood Palladium) was cancelled.

RunDMC have never been in gangs. Catholic school boys gone rogue? Nah! They are and were rap royalty, kings from Queens and just because violence broke out at their concert, that doesn't mean it was their fault.

It was at that time that the crossover hit single, "Walk This Way" (recorded with Aerosmith) was hot. That not only helped the hip hop trio experience mainstream pop success but if you check the footage on YouTube for those concerts, check and see if there is racial mixture in the crowd. You've got a bunch of black kids and white kids, side by side, having fun at a hip hop concert.

That's mostly what it was, from city to city and from state to state. And we had gone back to Cali five times after that Long Beach incident and there were no problems. But for some reason, the media chose to sensationalize the drama that the gangbangers brought to the concert. And that's not right. Let's be clear, that was a groundbreaking tour. It opened lots of doors and broke down many barriers.

There were sold out arenas throughout the United States for the *Raising Hell* concert. Then we crossed "the pond" (the Atlantic Ocean) and were in London for three weeks. We wound down the concert at Madison Square Garden, sold that out. Looking back at how much tickets cost nowadays, and to think that that concert at the Garden was only $17.50. Ha, the good ole' days.

Russell Simmons had flown in some Adidas executives from Germany, for the concert at the Garden. He had RunDMC instruct the crowd to raise their Adidas up in the air, and when the execs saw that, it was easy for Russell to negotiate a deal.

I experienced a lot of growth in those days. The album was so successful and we got a chance to go on tour and show the fans some love as well as capitalize on the fact that people were willing to pay to see their favorite rap artists.

Yes, there were a lot of shenanigans on that tour. With the combination of a bunch of young guys, nice hotels, girls, good food, publicity, fame and wealth that's not surprising at all. Some of the hotel rooms got so trashed, we were banned from some of them and had to sign in under aliases. Chalk it up as youthful indiscretions, but the main thing that I realized is: my dreams were coming true and I'd like to share with you more lessons I learned about making my dreams come true, so hopefully yours can too.

CHAPTER THIRTEEN

Be a Team Player

I got my start with organized ball by playing with the Hollis Biddies Basketball League back in the day. It was fun playing ball, learning to abide by the rules and regulations of the sport. I also got better and better. I was winning and scoring a lot.

We learned the responsibility of being at our games on time, and we had to take care of our uniforms. Those are lasting life skills that carry over and remain with me until this day. But there is one main skill that's tremendously developed when kids play sports, and I highly recommend emphasizing this to every child you know that plays sports: be a team player.

Being a team player is something I think is tremendously important in helping you to accomplish your dreams because more than likely, you won't be able to attain your goals on your own. Even if you do a lot of the work yourself, let's say you succeed. Who are you going to share your success with? Whoever that is is a part of your team.

More than likely, though, it's going to take a slew of people to help you make your dreams come true. So, it's best to be a team player and one of the things that can help you out is if you know your position.

Know Your Position

Team sports are rather different than going one on one. Everybody on the team has designated positions. That helps enable teams to run plays and strategize to best optimized talent on a team. In order to be effective on a team, it is important for a player to know his or her position.

Know where you're supposed to be and what you're supposed to do. Extremely important. Coaches run plays and have plans for each position. If you know your position, you are better able to play your position.

Play Your Position

Once you know where you're supposed to be and what you're supposed to do, it's on you to execute the game plays that your coach has communicated to you. There are certain things that you should be doing in your position that other people in their position are not supposed to do and vice versa.

If you have good players, a good coach and a good team, chances are you'll be able to run some of the plays your coach had in mind. And I think the sports adage: "Teamwork makes the dream work" is applicable here.

A play is something a coach may have in his or her mind, and they communicate that effectively to their players and the players do what is asked of them, it can have a desired outcome. But, as we well know, just because some know and play their position that does not mean they're going to win. And if they win, that does not mean they will win every time. But, it is good to know and play your position. It makes things easier for the team.

Be Coachable

Another thing that's helpful in being a team player is: being coachable. A coach is a coach for a reason. Usually, they have experience and can help guide you to play as a team. In many instances, coaches have studied plays and plotted and planned to have plays ready for teams.

Coaches usually have knowledge of each position, explaining what each player should do. So, you should go to a team trying to conform your abilities to the coach's coaching style. That means you have to check your ego and not allow anything you know (or think you know) stop you from flowing as you should with your coach and teammates. And once you get that going pretty well, another key element comes into the picture: practice.

Practice

I am thinking of a prominent ex-professional basketball player who had a famous beef with his coach about him not going to practice, being fined for not practicing. He would show up for games, but ditched practice all the time. When his NBA career ended (much sooner than he wanted), a lot of people didn't feel bad for him because of his antics regarding practice.

There's a type of arrogance associated with not practicing. Plus, it doesn't sit well with the rest of the team. Just showing up and giving your all to practice (or rehearsal) goes a long way. It further enhances your skills. And reinforces what you already know.

Practice is a good forecast of what you are going to when it's time to perform. If you don't practice, your performance will eventually reflect that. In most cases it will hurt you in the long run. So, make the time and take the time to practice. And if your team doesn't have regular practice, I suggest you link yourself with someone who knows the ropes, someone who's where you're trying to go in life and is willing to help you get there (with their advice). Get yourself a mentor.

CHAPTER FOURTEEN

Get a Mentor

As much as you'd like to think of yourself as unique, you're probably not so unique that there's nobody in the position in life you're heading for. And as the saying goes, "You don't have to reinvent the wheel." Somebody has done that already.

Where you're trying to go, somebody's "been there and done that." So why not benefit from their knowledge, experience and sometimes connections? I know for me, one of the best things that happened in my life is: I started out well-connected.

Friends in High Places

I didn't know it then, but I know it now. I was (and still am) in the midst of rap royalty. It doesn't get any better than going to grade school with Jam Master Jay, especially if your ambition is to be a DJ. Hanging with Russell Simmons all the time.... Who does that? Not that he's the most inaccessible dude, he isn't but way before he "blew up" to who and what he has become, I was hanging with him "on the regular" when I was a teen.

That's some really good exposure. But just because I'm in the midst of greatness that does not automatically mean that I am headed for greatness myself. Greatness does not rub off. Mastery usually comes when someone is trained and then works for quite some time at honing their skills.

As I stated in the intro of this book, I watched Mark, "the 45 King" backspinning. That left an impression on me. And I picked up some of those skills from him. But I mostly learned a lotfrom Davy D. And I'd be dead wrong if I didn't give props to my sister wholet me use her equipment to practice back in tha' day. I kept going and I suggest you do the same, taking into consideration certain things to look for when you seek out a mentor.

What Should You Look For

First of all, make sure you follow someone who knows where they are going. You want someone with skills and knowledge that they're willing to share with you – the knowledge (the information, and the know-how) plus to enhance your skills, the steps you need to take to acquire those skills.

You want someone who's going to teach you what they know. But you have to make sure it's a person who's cool with you shining. If they get all bent out of shape when you start getting better and better, and people show you more and more attention, you might be in for some bumps along the road. Make sure the mentor promotes and encourages you.

Don't Be Gullible

People who are successful usually have limited time. They're busy doing what made them successful. So make sure you have something you can bring to the table that can in some way be a contribution, valuable or worthwhile to the prospective mentor. I say that with caution because sometimes some experts in their chosen fields prey upon novices and/or people trying to gain access to their field.

The saying, "You don't get something for nothing" might ring true in your search for a mentor. Even if you can assist your mentor by helping to lighten their workload by some skill you have, try to see what you can do that will be helpful.

Not every mentor is crooked. As a matter of fact, plenty are not. And not everyone who mentors is looking for something in return. But, bear in mind, "time is money." Taking your mentor out for something as simple cup of coffee might go a long way, especially if your mentor is always on the giving end.

Consider the time and value of the information you receive from that person and see if you would like to continue to get information from that source. If so, nurture a mentor/mentee relationship and don't take it for granted. If not, seek another source for relevant knowledge and tips.

You're building a team of people who will be along various parts of your journey. A mentor is major and you must also consider other people who are within your circle.

CHAPTER FIFTEEN

Surround Yourself with Positive People

Have you ever heard the saying that "your network determines (or reflects) your net worth"? It's true so it would be best if you surround yourself with positive people who are already where you are trying to go in life, or at least on their way in a positive direction.

You're on the path, trying to make your dreams come true. And once you're really serious about it, you inevitably come to the point of looking at the people who are in your midst. Think about it. You might have some nice guys (and gals) around you, but are they negative influences?

Constructive

Haven't seen one for a while, but back in the day, there was such a thing as an Erector Set. It was a type of toy that consisted of beams, nuts, bolts, wheels, pulleys, gears and small electric motors. That thing kept (and keeps) kids busy for a long time. Something that reminds me of it, in a building kind of way, is Lego. Those toys are for the purpose of construction, building up. And you should think about that as you evaluate who is in your midst. Are they constructive?

Are they building up? Are they adding to what you're trying to do? Or are they ripping stuff up and pulling stuff apart? Does it seem like you're at a demolition site once certain people are around? You have to take that into consideration because it can have an effect on your energy level and productivity. And you are trying to make your dreams come true.

Purposeful People

People who seem to go places in life seem to have a sense of purpose. They're progressive, moving in a positive direction. It seems like purposeful people are always making plans, have places to go, things to do – always on the move. They tend to do positive things in life – and yes, money's important but it's not always about money.

I know people who seem on-point with purpose tend to be more positive. They're not wishy-washy. Those tend to be the more determined people in my midst. Not only is it important for you to spot those types of people, but you need to be one yourself.

Have a Sense of Direction

Do you know where you want to go in life? Do you know how you're going to get there? If you have already given those things some thought, how's it working out for you? If it's not, that's where help from positive people can be helpful in getting you onto a positive path.

If you're just aimlessly wandering through life, your days will be filled with useless activities and you won't have a serious regard your life, time and money. Take some time to think about where you're trying to go, much like planning a trip.

If you were going to go to another state, you would have to figure out where you're going, first of all. Next, you have to figure out how you're going to get there. How much does it cost? What are you going to do? Plot and plan.

One of the best things to do is chat with people who have been to your desired destination. Same holds true with pursuing your dreams. Chat it up with someone who has been where you're trying to go.

A Word of Caution

If you are pursuing a career or doing projects within the music and/or hip hop world, although someone may come across as positive to you, make sure you know who you're dealing with before you enter into anything legal or binding. It's kind of like you were warned when you were a little kid (if you were warned): Don't talk to strangers!

Well, not to that extreme but get to know who you're dealing with. Use your common sense and verify people are who they say they are. Yes, there are plenty of positive people out there who could possibly help your dream materialize.

You've just got to be on the path, pursuing your dream and sooner or later you'll meet them – if you haven't already. And even with positive people in your midst, that does not ensure your success. So, I highly recommend that you make alternate plans just in case your dreams don't come out precisely as you would like.

CHAPTER SIXTEEN

Have a Back-Up Plan

Follow your dreams but have a back-up plan. That's does not mean you're planning for failure. It's just to better prepare yourself if your dreams do not come true right away or if you get to the point where your dreams come true and you find out deep down inside, that's not what you really want.

Keep Your Options Open

There are a series of choices you will make along the path of having your dreams come true. So, it's best if you don't burn any bridges. Keep your options open. It gives you flexibility to maneuver so you don't feel boxed in or feel confined.

Yes, I've been living my dreams but a number of times throughout the years, I've had to make adjustments and do other things to sustain myself and support my family because at the end of the day, life is not just one big party. So, a DJ is not needed every day of the week. I've done a whole host of different thing to fill in the rest of the days of the week.

Learn New Things

As you're out and about in your day to day living, keep your eyes open for opportunities to learn new things related to what you like to do. You might be doing one particular thing in line with what you're dreaming about doing. And perhaps you're not quite there yet. Like if you're learning how to DJ, first of all keep your eyes open for when you can get a chance to see someone else DJ, up close and personal.

How do they choose their music? How do they get their paid gigs? Can you tag along and help out? Try to be a sponge and gain other information so you can have other things you can do within the realm of your interest.

Say if it's culinary, you should volunteer your time and go with a chef as they do an event. Perhaps you can help prepare the food, chop up the vegetables and fruits. See how the food is arranged. If you like taking pictures, maybe you might not end up being a master chef but how about a food photographer?

As you learn new things, try to angle what you've learned into an employable/marketable skill. That would put you in a better position to be in an environment where you'll most like be able to live out your dreams. What you actually end up doing will usually not be based on a single decision but if you trace your life today you will realize that where you are today is based on a series of decisions over the course of time. So, I suggest that you make wise decisions.

Make Wise Decisions

Talent and ambition are not the only factors that come into play in determining whether or not you will be successful in making your dreams come true. The day to day choices you make have a way of paying the path for your future.

The more decisions you make in line with your dream or in the ballpark of your dream, the more likely you will end up where you are trying to go. Again, plans sometimes fall through. But if you have plans in place as you face disappointments and setbacks, it will be easier for you to navigate yourself until you get to do what you'd like to do.

Decision making, repeatedly leads you to formulate habits. Once you establish a good pattern, your success is just about inevitable. It's just a matter of time. So, go forward, wisely heading in the direction of your dreams and realize your dreams can come true.

I have had tremendous success in my life since childhood. It hasn't been one success right after another. There have been some down times. Yes, there have been some lows. There have been some setbacks. I've lost some loved ones and dear friends along the way but that doesn't mean I should stop or slow down, neither should you. I keep going, and so should you.

Those people who I've loved and lost would want me to keep moving forward. So, I am. I'm gaining new ground, still plugging away at my dream. Why? Because I have new dreams. I have a great past. I've lived to see lots of my dreams come true but guess what? That's not it. Seems like I'm just getting started and the best is yet to come.

FINALE

The Best Is Yet to Come

I had the great fortune of growing up in the midst of rap and hip hop royalty. And have been able to participate on the hip hop scene in a groundbreaking way. But, while I hold what happened in the past near and dear to my heart, I am as equally enthused about what I am into and getting into.

I own my own production company, Don't Sleep Productions, and I am overseeing a young teenage rapper from Georgia whose video tribute to the Green Bay Packers became a viral hit on YouTube with over a million views, almost overnight. JBYRD is on the rise. Remember that name.

I am also still on the DJ scene. From 2008 – 2013, I was the touring DJ for Faith Evans and I was recently the Resident DJ at Las Vegas' Wynn Hotel club, Surrender and Encore Beach Club.

I am on the college lecture circuit as well. I've given some lectures at Full Sail University in Orlando, Florida and Kennesaw State in Georgia and am looking to expand my lecture itinerary.

Other books in the works are: Hip Hop and It Won't Stop: Because It's Big Busine$$; Over a Decade with the Beastie Boys; and the Hollis Crew. So, the best is yet to come. As a matter of fact, here's a sneak peek of my next book, More Than a Decade (with the Beastie Boys).

EXCERPT FROM UPCOMING BOOK:
More Than a Decade (with the Beastie Boys)

INTRODUCTION

One of My Best Decisions

When I was just 16 years old, my late "brother from another mother," Jam Master Jay of RunDMC recommended me to Russell Simmons as the Beastie Boys' replacement DJ for Doctor Dre – *not* the well-known record producer Dr. Dre who helped spawn the careers of Snoop Dogg, Eminem, 50 Cent, the Game, Kendrick Lamar and many others – but the one who co-hosted *Yo! MTV Raps* as a VJ (video jockey) with Hollis Queens native, Ed Lover.

At first, I was a bit hesitant. This was back in the pre-Vanilla Ice, Eminem or Macklemore days. White kids were not known for rap. They did not have a strong and commanding presence on the hip hop scene.

I thought about it for a little while and decided to give it a shot and I am so glad that I did. Who knew that those kids – mind you, I was a kid myself, at the time, but those kids (Michael "Mike D" Diamond; Adam "MCA" Yauch – RIP, my dude; and Adam "Ad Rock" Horowitz would go on to make the dent in hip hop that they did.

On top of being rappers, each of them played instruments: Mike D (drums); MCA (bass) and Ad Rock (guitar). The Beastie Boys could hold their own rapping and ended up breaking records and shattering color barriers.

As the "white rappers" on RunDMC's*Raising Hell Tour*, the Beastie Boys carved a niche for themselves and I was part of that team. They were legit rock stars, playing their heavy metal and punk rock and making good raps to go along with them. Of course, the DJ kept beats flowing.

The Beastie Boys debut album "License to Ill" was a worldwide sensation – and that was before all of this social media. They sold 9 million in the US, alone. It was the best selling rap album of the 80s and the first rap album to go to #1 on the Billboard Album Chart.

It was definitely their record label, Def Jam's, fastest selling debut album. And the success of the "License to Ill" album prompted the Tour which took us around the world. Back in 1995, ticket sales for arena tours here in the United States sold out in minutes.

So, I'm glad I decided to take what I thought was a temporary gig, to DJ for the Beastie Boys on *the Raising Hell Tour*. It ended up being my job for the next 12 years. This kid from Hollis got to see the world and became so deeply entrenched in the Beastie Boys' world.

Now, they were known for their success as a rapping rock group but they were young and acted their age. The paradoxical nature of the Beastie Boys was captured by an insulting title for a Rolling Stones magazine article about the License to Ill Album, "Three Idiots Create a Masterpiece."

Far from idiots, the Beastie Boys were young American kids on a seemingly endless vacation and if you weren't there, you would hardly believe what happened.

UP NEXT: Chapter One (Illin')

ABOUT THE AUTHORS

Wendell "Hurricane" (Cane) Fiteis a hip hop DJ, producer and rapper from Hollis, Queens who grew up as childhood buddies with the late **Jam Master Jay** of **RunDMC**. He got his start as a member of the group **Solo Sounds** with **Davy DMX** and as a bodyguard on **Run DMC**'s *Raising Hell Tour,* the same tour he went onto be a permanent DJ for **the Beastie Boys**for the next decade, plus. He was also a part of a group called **The Afros** and recorded three solo albums. **Cane** currently runs his own production company, *Don't Sleep Productions,* and is overseeing the career of a young teenage Georgia rapper **JBYRD,** whose video tribute to the **Green Bay Packers**became a viral hit, with over 1 million YouTube views, almost overnight. Recently, **DJ Hurricane** was resident DJ in Las Vegas at the **Wynn Hotel** club, Surrender and Encore Beach Club. From 2008 to 2013, he was the touring DJ for **Faith Evans. Hurricane** also lectures at colleges, including Full Sail University in Orlando and Kennesaw State University in Georgia.

Wiley "Chase" Griffin, Philadelphia, Pennsylvania native is creator or "Chase the Shark" Children's book series which includes "Flies Like a Bird" and "Hungry as a Bear."Currently employed by the City of Philadelphia is a proud father and foster parent whose love for hip hop reaches back for decades. Chaseis currently working with **Cane** on "Hollis Crew."

Jean Givan, born in Jamaica, NY and raised in Hollis, Queens, has been a hip hop lover since childhood. Exposure to poetry, reading and a love for learning came early to Jean through her mother's influence. Jean has a degree in English from Syracuse University and has utilized her literary prowess to help others with their written correspondence, school papers, theses, books and has written her own book: "21 Tips for Making It Out of Your Tough Times." Jean has worked (as script supervisor) on music videos (with **Jill Scott**and **Pharoahe Monch,** *Still Standing* and **Xavier Lewis,** *Give Back),* short films and full length feature films (including *Bad Parents,* starring **Jeaneane Garafalo, Christopher Titus and Michael Boatman)**

17990503R00031

Made in the USA
San Bernardino, CA
22 December 2014